Cryptocurrency

A Comprehensive Introduction To Cryptocurrencies, Including Cryptocurrency Mining And Cryptocurrency Trading

(How To Profitably And Securely Invest)

Marlon Kaiser

TABLE OF CONTENT

Introduction 1
Mindset For Crypto-Trading 5
Crypto Currency's Origins 22
The Beginnings Of Bitcoin 25
How To Recognize Potential Cryptocurrency Projects 39
The Blockchain Of Virtual Currencies 44
Most Popular Cryptocurrencies 55
The Crypto Market 86
A Brief Overview Of Cryptocurrency 99
How To Begin Investing In Cryptosurrensu . 110

Introduction

Hello to all my readers. I hope you all are investing safely, & wisely? Today let me tell you one short and interesting story that will most definitely be of value to you.

Surely you have all seen movies numerous times in your lives? In older films, there was a prevalent notion that kidnappers would abduct the children of wealthy people, or even their enemies, and then demand ransom from the victim. Today, as we enter the era of data, this kidnapping has taken on a new guise.

Today data is being abducted!

What do modern hijackers do? They gain access to your device, encrypt your data, and then demand a ransom in order to decrypt your data. Because data is now our most valuable asset.

The significance of data can be deduced from the fact that we sign up for Ponzi schemes to obtain gratis data. People use public Wi-Fi to access their private accounts because it is free. These crimes are intensifying to the point where hackers are now sending victims links to purchase bitcoins and sending them as ransom. Even Bitcoin accounts lack security. Neither are the servers from which people purchase crypto currencies, nor is the network where bitcoin trading occurs.

Today, I will reveal every detail I know about bitcoin hacking.

Today, investors from all over the globe are willing to purchase bitcoins. It is also practiced by a significant number of average citizens. This has fueled the growth of numerous blockchain and cryptocurrency-related firms.

Even more crypto currencies are being introduced to the market; an influx of unanticipated enterprises is observed. Despite this, many investors continue to be ignorant of security-related issues.

Bitcoin was introduced in 2009 as a decentralized alternative to third-party intermediaries. It had a decentralized structure. Therefore, it will not be overlooked. There will be no administrators who will be responsible for resolving impending disputes. In the case of fiat currency, the government is responsible for all issues and disputes.

The peer-to-peer nature of crypto currency has fueled its adoption. And among those, bitcoin was the most heavily promoted. This contributed to bitcoin's utter dominance of the cryptocurrency market. A public ledger is used to record all transactions.

These expose your information to the public and attract cybercriminals.

Mindset For Crypto-Trading

Everyone desires a higher income. This is the reason why commerce and investment are such desirable aspects and even more desirable careers. Many individuals must engage in trading and will fail. When assets advance in a straight upward direction, the majority of markets enter extreme conditions.

"I'm quitting my job to become a full-time entrepreneur" and "It's easy money" are common self-made fantasies. This can result in situations they are unsure of how to handle. Their lack of preparation and knowledge of the market cycle prevents them from purchasing repeatedly until their capital is depleted and the assets are sold at a substantial loss.

As with any pastime or profession, preparation must be undertaken prior to engaging. The majority of startups are unprepared to work hard and understand how the market functions. If you want to excel at something, you must devote countless hours to study. Practice improves performance.

I will instruct you on how to begin in this insane world, not how to become a nerd.

Learning is Profit.

Would you wager on the proposition if someone told you they would pay you $500,000 for a free throw in basketball, but you would have to pay them $25,000 if you forgot? Certainly, if you were a professional basketball player with countless hours of practice. However, if you have never shot a basketball before, you will decline the offer because 99.9% of individuals with no basketball experience will miss a shot.

This is precisely the case with commerce and investment. There is so much to comprehend, and everyone desires to begin making money immediately. It causes people to blindly follow random cartoon characters exchanging "calls" on Twitter or to leap into every large pump they see without understanding what is happening.

Unaware of what they are doing, many people lose a great deal of their fortune by exposing themselves and taking significant financial risks. Imagine telling a friend that you lost $10,000 due to a tweet about a fictional animal. It sounds absurd, doesn't it?

Picking and choosing indications

It can be difficult to determine where to begin studying markets. Here are my recommendations for initial destinations.

You likely already use Twitter. Follow accounts that share multiple perspectives on assets. You desire content that is well-reasoned and demonstrates logical reasoning.

Follow no one who constantly shares provocative reverse objectives and never mentions risk management. These comments are not helpful. You seek out posts that provoke thought. Emotions will only hinder you, whereas thoughts will increase your likelihood of success.

Before you commence trading,

If you are looking for fake trading or investing codes, you have come to the incorrect place. You will never receive a simple response because there is no simple method to study the markets. To conquer them, you must labor diligently and study independently.

Here is critical information that will help you outperform other market participants.

Understand market dynamics

What exactly is a bull market? How do they function? What is the ending? What exactly is a bear market? How do they function? What is the ending?

Gain knowledge of the psychology of the market cycle. You can use it to gauge your own emotions in the market as well as the emotions of others. It has the potential to be a potent tool in the overall market if used appropriately.

Where can you discover everything about them? Google is the optimal solution.

Once you have a firm grasp of market cycles, you can shift your attention to market structure.

Market structure is one of the most valuable pieces of knowledge for long-term investments. It can also be beneficial for short-term traders such as day traders.

I suggest examining the Wyckoff submission, Wyckoff distribution, and resubmission processes. The information they provide will entirely alter your chart's presentation.

It is not sufficient to simply recognize these patterns visually. I recommend reading in detail about what each stage of these schematics represents, why they occur, and how volume plays a crucial role in the structure.

Once you discover the average cost of dollars inside and outside these structures, you will feel like a genius.

The most essential thing is not to attempt to purchase or sell at the optimal bottom or peak. You will squander a great deal of time if you plan down or up instead of learning to recognize it. Remember that we enter these markets for financial gain. The only method to earn money is to generate a profit and store it in a hardware wallet. Become accustomed to earning a profit. You can become a successful trader or investor once you become accustomed to it.

Successful traders will never cease their education

My final bit of advice is to express your thoughts. There is always much to learn, and the only way to learn from others is to express your ideas publicly and to ask questions of more knowledgeable individuals. I had many useful mentors when I first began. I wouldn't be a full-time businessman if it weren't for the invaluable advice they gave me.

Getting Started

Create an account on a charting platform, such as Trading View or Trend Spider, and practice charting on your own. Real-time charting is where everything takes place. This is an excellent environment for trial and error learning.

Don't be frightened to be mistaken; everyone has been an idiot before. We all began our educations with no prior knowledge. You must have conviction, and until you achieve this level of confidence, you should be cautious with your capital.

Before beginning the game, you should study extensively and in-depth. And you must remember that you will not become wealthy on your very first night of trading. It will require countless hours of leisure time to eliminate it. Set some objectives, be trustworthy, and don't be hesitant to fail.

The proper frame of mind for Crypto-Trading

For the remainder of this chapter, you will be provided with distinct guidelines for permanently overcoming difficult cryptocurrency trading.

The appropriate mindset for trading cryptocurrencies is one that is calm and indifferent to crypto markets. To lose requires the same mental strength as to succeed. You do not repay the trade, and prior to entering the market, you anticipate every possible crypto trade.

You do not consider your results to be personal. You are solely liable for each cryptocurrency transaction, which you estimate after each trade closes.

Your Brain Is Vital

The harsh reality is that you cannot succeed in cryptocurrency trading without a trader's mindset.

Regardless of how confident you are in your business plans and crypto strategies, every time you trade a cryptocurrency you take a risk.

You can spend years searching for superior crypto trading strategies. You can define your risk management and accept a higher reward-to-risk (RTR) ratio. But without mindfulness, your relationship with cryptocurrency trading will be volatile and quick.

First Chapter: Cryptocurrency

Cryptocurrency is a virtual currency that employs cryptography to secure every transaction. Because of this security feature, it is nearly impossible to counterfeit this type of currency. Satoshi

Nakamoto, the creator of Bitcoin, which was the first cryptocurrency, did not intend to establish the so-called digital currency. In 2008, Nakamoto claimed to have created a "Peer-to-Peer Electronic Cash System," and in 2009, he announced the release of Bitcoin, an electronic cash system that precludes double-spending. Bitcoin is entirely decentralized, with no central server or authority.

Bitcoin was the first virtual currency to operate online, launching in 2009 under the alias Satoshi Nakamoto. As of February 6, 2016, there are approximately 15.2 million Bitcoins in circulation. Cryptocurrency is identical to traditional currency in that it can be stored, spent, and even invested. Due to the fact that virtual currency lacks a central repository, it can be lost in the event of a system failure if a backup copy does not exist. Cryptocurrencies are intended to reduce the issuance of currency. Bitcoin, the first cryptocurrency, has a total maximum supply of 21 million BTC. In other words, there are only 21 million Bitcoins that can be mined; once Bitcoin miners release this total amount of BTC, the supply will be exhausted.

'Mining' is required to obtain a digital currency, which others use to trade. No one knows who Satoshi Nakamoto is, or if it is a group or a single person.

What is Cryptocurrency Mining?

As a novice, you may be confused by the term 'Mining'; to illustrate this in a straightforward manner, consider golds and how they are mined. But before you purchase a tangible shovel and mattock, let me explain how virtual mining works. Cryptocurrencies such as Bitcoin are extracted using computers. To add a new block to the blockchain, mining necessitates the use of specialized processors that can solve complex mathematical problems. Anyone with internet access and the necessary equipment can participate in bitcoin mining and earn bitcoin rewards.

The difficulty of mining depends on how much effort you put into your network. To begin mining bitcoins, you must have all the necessary apparatus for an efficient and profitable mining process.

Things you require:

1. Acquire a Mining Rig Some choose to customize their own mining rigs, while others frequently invest in the most effective mining rigs.

2. Bitcoin Pocket WalletYou can think of this as an online wallet where you can securely store your bitcoins, etc. After signing up for a wallet, be careful to obtain your wallet address, which is a

long string of numbers and letters. In order to safeguard your coins, you must record your wallet's address on paper or use an external storage device as a backup in case your computer fails. So why must you do this? Simply stated, if you don't know your wallet address, when your computer crashes, all of your bitcoins will be lost forever.

Locate a Mining Pool A mining pool is a group of Bitcoin miners who aggregate their computing resources to obtain more Bitcoins. Joining a pool will result in a simpler and more compact algorithm to solve. However, before deciding to join a pool, a few factors must be considered, and these questions must be answered clearly.

• What is the pool's reward system? • What is the stability of the pool?

• What are the withdrawal fees and charges? • How simple is it to withdraw funds?

• How often do they discover a block?

4. Mining Program Choose a software based on the hardware you are employing - when using GPUs and FPGAs, you must use a host computer with the standard bitcoin wallet and the mining software installed. Consider your OS (Operating System) as well; for Windows, the best software is Bitcoin Miner and BTCMiner; for Linux, consider CG Miner BFG Miner and EasyMiner; and for Mac OS, RPC Miner is the best option.

The mining software will instruct the hardware to perform the mining task.

5. Start Mining Connect your miner and turn it on, then enter the mining pool, username, and password to begin the

mining process. Once setup, you are now able to process your first Bitcoin reward.

First-Rate Wallets 1. Coinbase This online wallet was founded in 2011 by Brian Armstrong and Fred Ehrsam. In October 2013 the company launched purchase and sell bitcoin services. This application facilitates cryptocurrency exchanges for Bitcoin, Ethereum, Litecoin, and Bitcoin Cash, among others. According to their website, this cryptocurrency has already facilitated 10 million customers and processed $50 billion worth of digital currency exchanges.

2. Electrum This is a prominent Bitcoin wallet available online. It is advantageous for both novices and professionals – Electrum prioritizes quickness and simplicity while consuming few resources. Using remote servers, this electronic wallet can

manage complex Bitcoin system components. If you lose your online wallet due to a computer malfunction, you can easily retrieve it using a secret phrase.

3. Trezor Trezor is the first hardware wallet on the market to include a passphrase. The passphrase feature protects the owner's funds should they lose the device. Trezor is a small device designed to prevent online access of private keys.

4. Nano Ledger S This wallet allows you to store the majority of prominent cryptocurrencies. It has a unique feature that enables two types of currency to be stored in the same wallet, unlike other wallets that only allow one.

Crypto Currency's Origins

Before the emergence of Bitcoin, numerous individuals and organizations explored the concept of electronic payment and digital currency. In the 1980s, computer scientist and cryptographer David Chaum proposed the concept of anonymous electronic currency, which he termed "ecash." His work established the groundwork for the development of digital currencies, but the first electronic cash systems were not deployed until the 1990s.

DigiCash, a corporation founded by Chaum in 1990, was one of the earliest and best-known examples of electronic cash. DigiCash used cryptography to develop a secure and anonymous system for online payments, but the company struggled to gain traction and ultimately declared bankruptcy in 1998.

Despite these initial setbacks, the concept of digital currency continued to develop and acquire popularity. In the late 1990s and early 2000s, several other digital currency systems, including e-Gold, Liberty Reserve, and PayPal, were developed. These systems enabled users to make online payments, but they were centralized, indicating that a single entity controlled them.

Enter Bitcoin. In 2008, a person or group using the alias "Satoshi Nakamoto" released a white paper describing Bitcoin, a novel decentralized digital currency. Bitcoin, unlike previous digital currencies, was founded on a distributed ledger technology known as a blockchain, which enabled transactions to be recorded and verified in a secure and transparent manner without the need for a central authority.

In the history of cryptocurrencies, the founding of Bitcoin and the establishment of a decentralized network for peer-to-peer transactions marked a turning point. In the following chapter, we will examine the early years of Bitcoin and the adoption of the currency by a small but devoted community of enthusiasts.

The Beginnings Of Bitcoin

When Bitcoin was first introduced in 2009, a small but devoted group of enthusiasts saw the potential for a decentralized digital currency to disrupt the conventional financial system. These early consumers were attracted to the concept of a decentralized currency that offered greater privacy and security than conventional payment methods.

Despite its initial promise, Bitcoin adoption was initially sluggish. There were few places where it could be used as a legitimate form of payment, and many individuals were skeptical of the idea. However, as the network expanded and more people became aware of

Bitcoin, a number of transactions in the real world began to occur.

In May 2010, one of the earliest known Bitcoin transactions was the purchase of two pizzas for 10,000 Bitcoins. In the broad scheme of things, this may seem insignificant, but it marked the beginning of Bitcoin's emergence as a legitimate form of payment.

Over time, an increasing number of merchants began accepting Bitcoin as payment, and the number of consumers increased. In 2013, Bitcoin's value attained an all-time high, and mainstream media began to pay attention to it. This marked the beginning of Bitcoin's ascent to prominence as a decentralized digital currency poised to challenge traditional financial institutions.

In the following chapter, we will discuss the proliferation of alternative cryptocurrencies, or altcoins, as well as the concept of a decentralized application (DApp). In addition, we will investigate the emergence of initial coin offerings (ICOs) as a means of funding new initiatives.Chapter 2 Mining Bitcoin

Now that you have a basic understanding of crypto coins and how they came into existence, you want to know how you can get involved in mining and whether it's worth the time and money required to mine the necessary coins.

There are two methods to participate in the mining operation. The first method is to establish a bank of puzzle-solving processors and distribute them to the general populace in exchange for a reward. The second method is to join a pool that generates bitcoins and then split the reward for completing the task.

In order to determine the profitability of the endeavor, you must evaluate a number of parameters. It depends on where you reside, the price of your electricity, the price of the hardware you need, and your technological proficiency. The objective is, of course, to be able to program and configure the hardware to efficiently mine the Bitcoin-rewarding puzzle solutions.

In the forthcoming chapters, we will discuss all of the necessary components for determining this. For the time being, we will examine Bitcoin mining, which is unique to Bitcoin and not inherently applicable to other cryptocurrencies. There are similarities between various coins, but this is not always the case. However, the logic for determining them remains unchanged.

To comprehend the Bitcoin mining process, let's examine the components you must assemble in order to collect the reward.

What must be Resolved?

We had a brief discussion about this earlier, but it was only a passing glance. This will now be discussed in detail in relation to Bitcoin.

The Bitcoin algorithm presents a riddle that must be solved. Simply combine all the various components of a block, and then run it through a hashing algorithm. That will provide you with a hash.0 must fall within a given parameter.

Once a miner has grouped a number of transactions, he or she is free to select whichever transactions they desire or simply take them at random. Then, as expected, arrange them in a block. To solve the conundrum, they must add a number to the block and then hash the result. What is the quantity? Actually, it could be any number. Miners continue to estimate and attempt until they achieve the desired result.

The number is referred to as a nonce. There are multiple possible nonces for the block, and it may not always be the same nonce, as different miners use different transactions to produce a block. That will result in a unique hash for the combined nonce and block. Therefore, miners typically use random numbers as the nonce until they obtain the correct hash. On average, it takes the system approximately ten minutes to generate a block.

But do not be deceived by this. Even though it takes ten minutes, if you only have one piece of hardware, you will not be obtaining the reward every ten minutes. That is not how it works. It boils down to something known as the hash rate. In order to determine how much power you need and how many times you can hash in a given amount of time, we must examine your hashing power.

This may become perplexing, so let's examine it once more.

There is a substantial quantity of computing power within the Bitcoin universe. The entire Bitcoin network is conducting approximately twenty trillion hashes per second at the time of writing. That's a substantial amount of hashing capacity. Keep in mind that a hashing output is the result of executing the algorithm and converting the number of transactions into blocks.

The blockchain is the central component of a coin, particularly Bitcoin. Everything revolves around the blockchain and its continued existence. If miners do not organize the transactions into blocks, the entire system comes to a halt.

However, there is also a need to regulate the quantity of Bitcoin entering the market. There is a maximum number of bitcoins that can be in circulation. This amount is 21 million. Once that number is reached, no more bitcoins will be created, and the total supply will either remain at 21 million or begin to decrease over time.

How is it diminished? I am all too familiar with this. Back when Bitcoin was worth approximately $13, I had my wallet on a computer that crashed. I had approximately thirty coins in there, but I never bothered to retrieve them. I had not made a backup nor had I written down the private key. How do you suppose I felt as my bank account approached $20,000? Those coins that I had on my hard drive but never used are lost permanently, not only to me but to the entire community.

Thus, it is possible for coins to lose value over time. The coins, however, are divisible, so we can construct as many divisions as necessary. However, that comes afterward. For the time being, miners are only compensated in bitcoin until there are no more bitcoins to mine. This date and the number of coins that enter the market in a given year are fixed. This is accomplished by decreasing miners' compensation every few years. When first introduced to the market, miners received 50 BTC per transaction. Eventually, this decreased to 25, and is now 12.5 BTC per transaction. Bitcoin is designed to generate a block every ten minutes;

consequently, 12.5 BTC enter the market at this rate. In a day, that equates to approximately 1,800 new coins. This internal rate has been hard-coded into the system, and the miners' computers must operate at this rate to solve the block.

Currently, there are 16 million Bitcoin in circulation. It will have a maximum circulation of 21 million. That leaves just over four million to go. This is a point that you will not find online if you intend to enter the mining industry; therefore, you should read up and pay close attention!

There is a limit on how much can be mined, and this limit is hard-coded into the software. The software's developers determined precisely how much a CPU could produce at any particular time and the maximum amount of processing it could handle. In addition, they programmed into the software the amount of computing power distributed throughout the mining universe. Then, they would determine the difficulty of the required conundrum to solve the block. This is modified until the output is ten minutes.

The intriguing aspect of this is that the software of the currency controls the difficulty of the puzzles that the computers must solve. It is programmed to become more challenging as the computational power of the aggregate mining network grows. However, it is still expected to take ten minutes, so you can determine how much energy you require.

Before we proceed, we must review some information about hash and hash rate. Remember that hashes are simply a method for obtaining a random string of characters, regardless of their length.

Theoretically, you could run the municipal telephone directory through a hash function and obtain a hash. No matter what size it is, it must be run through an algorithm and, dependent on the algorithm, it always comes out the same size. Therefore, the resulting number is not a string of arbitrary digits; it is highly precise.

Everything that must be included in the block is specified. You must have the hash of the previous block and all the transactions you wish to include. Also, you must have the nonce; recall the number we discussed.

Now, let's examine the Bitcoin nonce closely to gain a clearer understanding of what's going on.

Bitcoin indicates that the final hash will always be 256 bits in length. They will specify how they want the cannabis to appear. You can only control the nonce, as you have no control over the remainder of the information in the block.

In the subsequent block, you input the hash from the previous block, the data to be included in this block, and a number called the nonce. The nonce is determined by guesswork. Because what you want to achieve is a specific type of hash at the end, and Bitcoin will tell you whether they want 30, 32, or 40 zeros in front. The number of leading zeros is a random occurrence because you are attempting random nonces.

This type of trial and error requires considerable effort. The processor is diligently searching for the nonce that, when added to the block, returns a hash conforming to the specified format, i.e. the number of leading zeros.

As soon as your processor receives the nonce, you send the entire block to the network, where Bitcoin can readily verify your proof of work. Because there is no other way you could have obtained the nonce without performing each step individually. Each time the block is executed with the nonce, it is hashed. Therefore, the quicker you hash, the more you can convert, and the quicker you can reach the desired hash output.

There are multiple profitable approaches to entering the mining market. Entering the mining business simply because you have a home PC or MAC and believe you can make extra money is not the best strategy, particularly if you are considering BTC mining. My recommendation is not to do so, and here is why.

How To Recognize Potential Cryptocurrency Projects

Considering the rapid expansion of the market, it may be difficult to choose the finest new cryptocurrency to invest in. However, investors may use the five strategies listed below to rapidly identify cryptocurrencies with high potential:

Pay attention to price potential

Price potential is the most important consideration when selecting the best cryptocurrency investment. This encompasses a variety of factors, such as the coin's current value and the market segment in which it competes, despite the fact that it may sound vague. By combining these variables, investors can guarantee that coins with limited price potential are avoided.

For instance, there is a high likelihood that investors will be interested in a new currency introduced in the rapidly expanding metaverse sector and featuring a unique selling proposition. To accomplish convergence, this strategy must be combined with other types of analysis.

Continually monitor market conditions

Finally, it is essential to pay close attention to the current state of the market when selecting the finest cryptocurrency to purchase right now. This is a fairly comprehensive strategy that includes analyzing the general economic climate, market regulation, and the possibility of "black swan" events.

The demise of FTX is an outstanding example of the need to consider market realities. Even though BTC and ETH were not directly affected by the incident, the contagion effect caused their values to decrease. Therefore, it is preferable to exercise perseverance and wait until the market has stabilized following a catastrophic event before investing.

Search for unique use cases

Innovative use cases distinguish the leading cryptocurrencies to invest in from the competition. This is essential because it provides investors with a compelling argument to choose their initiative over competing ones.

Learn About Cheap Coin Trading

The cryptocurrencies with the greatest profit potential are those that are presently undervalued. To define what comprises a "discount," which can be difficult and arbitrary, it is necessary to investigate the coin's utility, development team, and long-term goals.

It could be good or negative if a coin has a beautiful exterior but is priced very cheaply. The coin's low price may have resulted from a variety of factors, but if larger economic issues are to blame, there is the possibility of a return if conditions improve.

Participate in Social Media Platforms

Utilize social media networks if you are uncertain of what to invest in at the moment. Despite the apparent contradiction, social media sites are an excellent place to discover currencies and projects that are attracting the attention of retail traders.

This is exemplified by Dash 2 Trade and RobotEra, two initiatives that have already established robust communities on Twitter and Telegram. These communities are essential because they foster the growth of a solid demand base and lay the foundation for future price increases.

The Blockchain Of Virtual Currencies

Satoshi Nakamoto was the creator of the blockchain concept. It has progressed significantly since then, and the glory of blockchain is that it enables the distribution of digital information without its duplication.

The blockchain technology was initially designed for use with Bitcoin, but it is now also utilized with other cryptocurrencies.

It is presumed that Satoshi Nakamoto referred to a chain of blocks in his original white paper when he coined the term blockchain. The term blockchain was likely first mentioned in a conversation between Hal Finney and Satoshi on November 9, 2008. It is likely that the term entered common usage when the two words were combined to form blockchain.

Although not every cryptocurrency uses blockchain technology, the vast majority does. Blockchain is currently employed for a vastly broader spectrum of applications than just cryptocurrency. Its underlying principles are proving useful in a variety of industries. By comprehending the fundamentals of blockchain, including what it is and how it operates, you can appreciate the vast array of benefits it provides.

Reduced Transaction Costs – Since it is decentralized, there is no requirement for a third-party clearing house, which eliminates overhead and fees.

Security – The blockchain's cryptographic safeguards make all transactions extremely secure.

Anyone with access to a computer can view the information on a blockchain, allowing for complete transparency. This drastically reduces the likelihood of corruption.

Availability - The system operates by connecting thousands of distinct processors, known as Nodes. This ensures that even if some nodes depart or cease functioning for any reason, there will always be others available to maintain the system's functionality.

Reliability – The conventional method for sustaining databases was disorganized and prone to data loss, corruption, and error. It was challenging to share data, and frequently only one user could update the database at a time. Using blockchain technology, this is no longer the case. Every few minutes, new data created by anyone with access to the system is first validated and then updated. This introduces new data blocks to the chain. This data is accessible to everyone, but the encrypted portions are hidden from view, protecting your personal information.

Due to the rapidity of the blockchain verification process, the time required for transactions to be verified, reconciled, and cleared has been drastically reduced. This takes place within a few minutes. This is why so many organizations, including banks and financial institutions, are interested in blockchain technology.

The data stored on a blockchain ledger is publicly accessible. It creates a database that is accessible to everyone on the Internet. This is advantageous because the information is not stored in a single location, such as on a single server. It is stored on all network-connected devices, known as nodes. This effectively transforms it into a globally distributed database of information. This also makes it possible for members of the public to readily verify the ledger's records. Because it exists in multiple locations and does not have a centralized copy, it is nearly impossible for a criminal to compromise.

Traditional accounts and monetary transactions are maintained and recorded on a bank's central server. In order to make adjustments to a specific account, that account must be frozen while the account is updated and money is transferred in or out. When the procedure is complete, the account is unlocked and both sides of the transaction are visible in their respective accounts. Almost all databases operate in this manner at present, with very few exceptions. Anyone can access the blockchain ledger at any time and execute their own transactions on it. In order for these transactions to be considered valid, however, they must be validated by a third party using sophisticated encryption protocols.

Every 10 minutes, the blockchain network refreshes and reconciles all transactions. The resulting group of transactions is known as a block. The reason a block of information is so secure and unalterable is because an intruder would need to override the entire global network in order to alter any portion of the block. As each new block of information is added to the ledger, the ledger creates chains of blocks, making this theoretically possible but exceedingly unlikely in practice. Each new block contains some data from the previous block and a unique identifier that identifies it as belonging to that block. This is the origin of the term blockchain.

All the individual devices connected to the blockchain network are used to validate and transmit transactions. Individual devices are referred to as "nodes." These nodes (individual computers) create a powerful network, and each one serves as a distinct blockchain administrator. Due to the fact that each node joins the blockchain network voluntarily, it is a decentralized network in which no single user is in command. Nodes are incentivized to join the network in order to earn cryptocurrency coins; this process is known as "mining" and is accomplished by each "miner" solving complex mathematical riddles.

Some have compared cryptocurrencies to telephones or fax devices. If only one person in the entire world possesses it, it is useless. However, their maximum potential can only be realized when they are widely distributed.

Because the blockchain is a global network of computers with equal ability to manage the ledger (database), the technology is decentralized, as it is not controlled by a central authority. It operates on a strictly peer-to-peer (user-to-user) basis.

Currently, blockchain technology is in its infancy, but blockchain developers are in high demand as the applications for blockchain technology become more evident.

Currently, we rely on usernames and passwords to keep our digital information secure, and we know that these are not particularly difficult for hackers to crack, so the implementation of blockchain-based security is of great interest.

We have all heard of companies that have disclosed or lost personal data. If our data were decentralized using blockchain, these incidents would be impossible.

In the future, blockchain technology will facilitate vastly improved digital authentication methods, which will have applications in numerous industries. Smart contracts, the sharing economy (think Uber and Air BnB), production markets, crowdfunding, file storage, governance, identity management, auditing of supply chains, intellectual property protection, neighborhood microgrids, anti-money laundering, data management and registration of land titles, stock trading, and numerous other applications will undoubtedly be affected. It is truly the future.

The blockchain procedure is streamlined:

There is an update to the database. This transaction would be a sale or purchase of cryptocurrency tokens.

The transaction information, amount, and vendor and buyer details are transmitted to all nodes in an encrypted format.

The nodes examine and validate the data.

A unit is created.

The block is added to the distributed ledger.

Every 10 minutes, a new update occurs, adding a new block of data to the ledger's chain.

Each block contains elements from the preceding block. This assures that the block order cannot be altered, as the blocks would no longer be compatible.

Chapter overview:

In his white paper, Satoshi Nakamoto describes the creation of blockchain.

Bitcoin transactions were the first use of blockchain technology.

Blockchain's rising prominence is a result of its low cost, security, transparency, dependability, and speed.

Blockchains function by adding new data entries to a ledger. As additional blocks are added, they are connected, forming a block chain or blockchain.

Step one of the quick start guide: You can conduct additional investigation on this topic by consulting one of the numerous online guides. You can search for the article titled "How does blockchain technology work?" on websites such as www.coindesk.com.

Most Popular Cryptocurrencies

There are over a thousand cryptocurrencies in circulation. Nonetheless, only a handful of them are actively traded. Popularity of a cryptocurrency implies that it is simple to exchange and convert. Moreover, there is a greater possibility that its value will increase as a result of increased speculation. Speculation is what makes a cryptocurrency a more attractive investment option.

This section will examine the five most prominent cryptocurrencies on the market.

Bitcoin

Bitcoin is the most widely used digital currency. It is the trend-setter in the cryptocurrency universe. It has been actively transacting since 2009. 'Satoshi Nakamoto', an anonymous pseudonym, devised it. It now represents approximately 45 percent of the complete cryptocurrency market. Bitcoin's blockchain technology allowed it to flourish despite the failure of numerous prior attempts at cryptocurrencies. The distributed ledger system prevented double expenditures. Early adopters of the so-called 'dark internet' ('darknet') were individuals who desired anonymity. These individuals engaged in money laundering, cybercrime, illegal trade, and other criminal activities. However, as a result of its rapid and less expensive transaction process, it came to be widely accepted for legitimate legal transactions.

Ethereum

Ethereum is the second most widely used digital currency. Vitalik Buterin developed Ethereum. Ethereum is so prevalent due to its adaptability. The 'programmable blockchain' is the driving force behind Ethereum's growth. A blockchain that is programmable enables developers to construct their own blockchains. With the ability to construct their own blockchain, programmers are able to create their own apps and ICO (Initial Coin Offering)-launched versions of Ethereum coins.

ICOs on Ethereum have increased its market capitalization. Numerous entrepreneurs have been able to raise funds for their own Ethereum initiatives as a result. Ethereum's programmable blockchain and custom Ethereum applications have made it more attractive to financial institutions than Bitcoin.

Ethereum's so-called 'Smart Contracts' (self-executing conditional payments) are another popular feature. This is because, unlike Bitcoin, the Ethereum blockchain validates not only a collection of accounts and balances, but also 'States'. States involve intricate contracts and programs. Ethereum's smart contract is DAO. The disadvantage of this adaptability is that it facilitates hacker activity. Since the initial hijacking of its original DAO, however, Ethereum has been able to develop sophisticated security features. It developed more secure DAO variants, including DigixDAO and Augur.

Ethereum has developed Proof of Stake (PoS) as a transaction verification system to deter intruders. This is significantly more efficient than the traditional 'Proof of Work' (PoW) employed by Bitcoin and numerous other cryptocurrencies.

Ethereum is currently more of a family of cryptocurrencies than a single cryptocurrency.

Ripple

XRP is the native cryptocurrency of Ripple. Ripple differs from other cryptocurrencies in that it is primarily a network designed to process IOUs rather than a cryptocurrency. Thus, unlike Bitcoin, Ripple serves as an anti-spam network token rather than a medium for value storage and exchange. As a result, Ripple does not use blockchain to establish transaction consensus. It employs an iterative consensus procedure, which makes it faster but also more vulnerable to hacking attacks.

Ripple advertises itself as a "immediate, secure, and less expensive global financial transaction system with no chargebacks." This is why many financial institutions are experimenting with Ripple in an effort to reduce the expense of international clearinghouses and exchange systems. Among notable financial institutions are the main banks in Japan.

Litecoin

The first alternative coin (altcoin) to Bitcoin was Litecoin. It became known as 'digital silver' as Bitcoin assumed the position of 'digital gold'. Litecoin came up with an algorithmic system (scrypt) that is faster than Bitcoin's (which employs SHA256) and allows for the mining of a greater number of tokens. It was designed to be a 'lighter' Bitcoin mining alternative. It accomplished this feat by being mined four times quicker than Bitcoin. With 84 million tokens, its volume is also four times that of Bitcoin.

As the cost of Bitcoin mining has increased, it has become much more difficult to mine. Currently, ASICs are required for Bitcoin processing. ASICs are highly specialized and expensive devices. This renders Bitcoin mining the domain of a handful of large-scale miners, as small-scale miners are pushed out of the market. In contrast, GPUs are not required to mine Litecoin. GPUs are affordable and inexpensive. Modern desktops, laptops, and gaming devices feature potent GPUs. Thus, Litecoin remains genuinely decentralized while Bitcoin becomes increasingly centralized.

Several other cryptocurrencies were created using its codebase as a foundation. Among these are Feathercoin and Dogecoin.

At the time of its inception, it was the second largest cryptocurrency. However, it was eventually replaced by Ethereum.

Litecoin is still actively mined as a form of Bitcoin insurance.

Monero Monero is marketed as the most private and anonymous cryptocurrency. It has strict privacy requirements. The transaction is almost impossible to trace. It utilizes the 'cryptonite' algorithm. This algorithm was created to incorporate missing Bitcoin features. It utilizes the ring-signature concept. Thus, the coins are 'mixed' at the protocol level, rendering the transaction untraceable. Monero was the first Bitcoin clone that was not pre-mined. It has spawned numerous other forms of crypto notes. Despite this, it remains the most popular anonymity coin.

Definition, Characteristics, and Classes of Blockchain

The number of cryptocurrency investors and enthusiasts has skyrocketed in recent years. However, non-specialists frequently halt at the innovation in the financial sector of transactions, not realizing that cryptocurrencies are merely the tip of the iceberg in terms of the variety of innovative applications offered by blockchain technology. To contextualize the new technology, it is necessary to begin with the distributed system concept depicted in Figure 2.

Figure 2 - System Types

The first illustration depicts a centralized one-to-many system, similar to our economic system, in which decisions and inputs are provided by a central institution that plays a prominent role in the network. The second connotation is that of a decentralized system; in this instance, consider an enterprise that, operating in diverse geographical contexts, grants strategic autonomy to its subsidiaries, thereby establishing multiple local centres of responsibility. The third classification is applicable to the blockchain, which is a distributed system. In this context, each participant of the network, known as a "node" in computer parlance, is placed on an equal footing with the other participants and participates with them in the process of will formation, based on the democratic majority formed by the approval of 50% plus one of the nodes.

To adequately clarify blockchain, it is necessary to provide multiple definitions.

In computer jargon, blockchain is defined as a decentralized and distributed communication protocol that employs cryptography; however, this definition has little explanatory value for the unwary.

Therefore, we continue on to the second definition, which describes the blockchain as a Peer-to-Peer (P2P) network architecture that serves as the foundation for numerous computer applications. P2P refers to a system in which each network participant (node) has the same weight and where nodes share responsibility. A P2P computer protocol is distinguished by the absence of hierarchies and centralized services or positions within the network.

Having clarified some of the technology's fundamental concepts, we can now provide a more pragmatic definition. As an implementation of the "Distributed Ledger", the blockchain is a decentralized, distributed, and encrypted ledger or database in which all interactions between network nodes are recorded in an immutable fashion5. This technology enables the transmission of both information and property via the internet, as is the case with cryptocurrencies.

According to "The Economist," a blockchain is a sequential spreadsheet of transactions that is continuously updated across a global network of computers and serves as a distributed ledger.

The supplied definitions provide an overview of the most essential characteristics of the technology.

Traceability

The database is composed of interconnected modules, such that all network operations are validated by the nodes that comprise it. In reality, these nodes perform a variety of tasks, including monitoring the operations/transactions of other nodes, ensuring the consistency of operations, and ultimately approving them.

Immutability

Each node that joins the network downloads and replicates the database, transaction history, and the entire transaction log. In order for a transaction to be present on the network and validated by it, it must be immutable unless it is resubmitted for approval.

Security

In addition to immutability, the system's security is ensured by the application of cryptography to transactions, a topic that will be discussed in detail in the following section of the chapter.

Security is also ensured by the fact that all database information is accessible to all network participants, who will have a complete history of all block operations.

This indicates how the database is disseminated across multiple computers (PCs) in a distributed system.

Clearly, such a Database Management System, compared to a database located locally or managed by a single subject, ensures reliability in data management and their preservation even in the event of a malfunction, as well as their confidentiality, protecting the data and the ledger containing them from unauthorized actions aimed at modifying them. Since the database is replicated on all nodes, if someone wanted to modify the information contained within it, he would need at least half of the computing capacity (computational) of all networked computers in order to correct it.

Since the introduction of Bitcoin in 2008, when blockchain technology was released for the first time, its implementations have grown and their degree of customization has increased.

At this juncture, a more comprehensive understanding of the technology is required to define the various types of blockchain.

Open Blockchain

Also known as "permissioned distributed ledgers" or simply "Public," they are Peer-to-Peer networks that are accessible to all potential participants and have no central authority. This architecture enables all network nodes to actively contribute to database data updates and access a copy of all database operations. In fact, each node can partake in the consensus process, i.e., control and approve the transactions that comprise a given block before it is added to the chain (block-chain).

In contrast to a centralized system in which a single entity guarantees transparency and compliance, in a public blockchain these characteristics are assured by the combination of computer problem solving and economic incentives.

In this context, the degree to which each network node can contribute to consensus formation is proportional to the computational capacity it can invest in the transaction approval process.

These networks are categorized as completely decentralized.

Exclusive Blockchain

In this type of network, the approval of operations, and therefore the process of consensus formation, is not required of the majority of system participants, but is instead delegated to an organization, which represents the central authority wholly absent in the previously described Public networks.

On the other hand, the chain management method is identical; in fact, the block management follows a specific order, but the central organization can restrict or allow public access to the database. Therefore, we are confronted with a centralized system that also includes a cryptographic verifiability system.

Blockchain Association

It identifies the network type in which the "consensus process" is conducted by a predetermined set of nodes. Additionally, in this context, the perusing of the blockchain can be public or restricted to a subset of network nodes.

This third form is partially decentralized because it is a hybrid between the trustless public blockchain network and the centralized "Private" blockchain network.

To conclude the general overview, it is important to revisit the categories of blockchain, highlighting the advantages and disadvantages of the "Public" and "Private" types.

In networks managed by a consortium or a specific organization (Private), the protocol is easily modifiable by these entities; in truth, the fundamental rules can be altered, as well as transactions and balances. Moreover, unlike "Public" networks, the validators that contribute to the formulation of the consensus are known. This reduces the risk of a system being attacked by network nodes with more than 50 percent plus one of the computing power.

The ability to restrict permissions to access the database provides a high level of confidentiality in private blockchains. The cost of transactions represents a further significant advantage. In

"Private" blockchains, transactions require the approval of a limited number of trustworthy nodes, resulting in lower transaction costs compared to public blockchains, where verification is performed by thousands of computers. Alternatively, a major advantage of the "Public" type is the protection provided to the system's users by the system's developers, who, by relinquishing their autonomy to independently make substantial changes to the protocol, sustain and strengthen the concept of "Trustless System."

Despite the advantages described above, there is no dominant typology; rather, the applicability of each depends on the intended use and context.

Data encryption and security

Previously, when defining blockchain technology, the term cryptography was mentioned multiple times; this section clarifies the concept.

Cryptography is the field of study that examines the process of encoding messages prior to their placement on a network, rendering the information unintelligible to anyone attempting to intercept it. This mechanism determines the exclusivity of the message's reading and comprehension by the recipient; through a decoding process, the information is made plain and understandable.6. Plaintext refers to the unencrypted portion of a message, while ciphertext refers to the portion that has been rendered unintelligible. Encryption is the process of converting plaintext to ciphertext, while decryption is the converse process.

Only a perfect cryptographic system can guarantee absolute privacy and confidentiality in a computer data exchange. In this context, there are two types of flawless encryption algorithms:

"Computational Secrecy" refers to an impregnable cryptographic system that takes into consideration the resources available to the cyber-attacker.

"Perfect Secrecy" refers to an encryption algorithm that is mathematically unbreakable.

Towards the two systems described above, a cryptographic algorithm tends to acquire its robustness. Moreover, there are two families of encryption functions:

Use-restricted cryptographic algorithms

The fact that the functions of encryption and decryption are unknown determines their operation. Consequently, the effectiveness of the algorithm derives from its secrecy.

Algorithms for general cryptographic applications

Unlike the previous algorithm, since the encryption and decryption functions are known, this algorithm is based on a pair of keys, one public and one private. The public key is accessible to everyone, whereas the private key is personal and must be kept covert.

As previously described, a cryptographic system must possess the following seven properties in order to guarantee message integrity and sender authenticity:

Informational reliability

This property ensures that messages cannot be altered without the appropriate authorization. In fact, a message's worth is determined by its consistency and honesty.

The digital signature is the most well-known mechanism for preserving the integrity of a message.

Accessibility to data

It ensures that the correct recipient receives the message, which is not evident given the numerous cyberattacks that tend to alter the availability of information in digital archives.

Confidentiality

It is the system property that guarantees and protects the confidentiality of the encrypted message.

Through the use of cryptographic algorithms, it is ensured that only the intended recipient can read the message, as only he has the necessary tools to decrypt it, ensuring the confidentiality of communications.

Non Rejection

The non-repudiation property of a system makes it impossible for the sender to deny transmitting the message. Digital signatures, a subset of electronic signatures, are associated with this property.

Key for symmetric encryption (private)

As described previously, the cryptographic algorithm enables the concealment, or encryption, of plaintext. This type of transformation is known as parametric because it requires the completion of a parameter, also known as a key.

In order to decipher a message, a user must possess the key in addition to knowing the encryption algorithm used in the transformation.

The simplest and earliest cryptographic algorithm is referred to as a "symmetric key" or a "private-secret key." The sender and recipient utilize the same private key for encryption and decryption in this system.

However, both the described procedure and the cryptographic algorithm to which it refers are susceptible to certain flaws. Due to the lack of security of the transmission channel, which necessitated encrypting the message, it is initially necessary for the parties to meet and concur on the secret key to be used. Second, this mechanism relies on the uniqueness of the key for each pair of users, resulting in the generation of an extremely large number of keys.

Asymmetric ciphering (public key)

With the introduction of "asymmetric" or "public key" cryptography in the 1970s, the defects exhibited by the symmetric cryptographic system were resolved.

According to this algorithm, every user possesses two distinct keys: one public and one private. The user provides the public key to those he wishes to communicate with, while the private key must be kept covert.

The public key enables the encryption of the message's content; the private key, on the other hand, enables the decryption of the message's content, which can only be performed by the proprietor of the same key (private).

This cryptographic algorithm therefore addresses the "symmetric" mechanism's inherent problem of communicating the secret key.

In order to elucidate the operation of the process further, we consider Bob and Alice's computer communication.

Bob must encrypt the message with Alice's public key in order to communicate with her, and only Alice, in possession of her private key, will be able to decrypt it.

Bitcoin's hashing algorithm

Within the Bitcoin infrastructure, cryptography plays a crucial role in several operations that will be covered in detail in the following sections, such as "Mining" and verifying the blockchain's validity.

However, cryptographic algorithms are also used to generate keys, Bitcoin addresses, and authorize transactions. The hash function is one of the most significant algorithms used in this context.

The hash function is a mathematical algorithm that maps data of arbitrary length to a fixed-length binary string known as a "message digest" or hash value.

This algorithm admits values of arbitrary length and returns values of fixed length, which are typically shorter. Various algorithms, SHA (Secure Hash Algorithm) being one of the most well-known, are used to achieve these results.

The primary characteristic of this function is that it is non-injective, which means that it cannot be reversed; the only method to return from output data to input data is to conduct "brute force research." This operation involves searching for a given value among all potential inputs in an attempt to find a match.

Several issues and difficulties with asymmetric cryptography, such as the key system (public and private) and addresses, are resolved by the Bitcoin protocol.

Regarding asymmetric encryption, as described in the preceding section, it should be noted that a communication's process can resolve in a manner distinct from that described.

The Crypto Market

Bitcoin Trading

There are two methods to begin active trading in a trade. One option has a cost advantage; therefore, it is recommended to begin trading with this option, particularly if you are a novice. The second option is accurate and provides a professional advantage, but it is quite expensive. The decision is never simple.

It is difficult for a beginner to determine which option to pursue. There are numerous factors to consider, but if you intend to commence slowly, remember to choose the most cost-effective option. In your initial foray into the cryptocurrency market, if you began with between 5 and 10 Bitcoin, moving online would not be prohibitive. Starting with that quantity, you will likely execute between three and five trades per day. At this time, the online exchange is acceptable.

Trading houses and online exchanges will allow you to execute trades and utilize trading instruments to find optimal buy and sell points. Several intermediaries offer this service for free with a minimum deposit.

You may also choose not to utilize an online trading platform and instead obtain the price feed from the Bloomberg Terminal. Bloomberg provides real-time quotes for the most popular cryptocurrencies, particularly the most recent ones. They may also enable you to chart all cryptocurrencies and provide the flexibility to program your strategy directly from your feed.

If you plan to engage in crypto trading on a long-term basis, you should purchase the necessary instruments. It is essential to research your options and potential costs.

If you decide to use the online system for rapid-fire transactions, you must have a reliable internet connection, as lag time is unacceptable at any trading level.

Trading Techniques

We will provide you with three trading strategies that you can employ when you begin trading cryptocurrencies. These three strategies will serve as the basis for other strategies you will learn as a beginner, allowing you to develop and improve your trading skills.

You should bear in mind that the market is in a constant state of flux – transactions are constantly taking place. With over 50 conceivable currency and fiat pairings, this can become a full-time occupation.

Purchase Dips

Dips are instances in which the price movement takes a momentary stride back after advancing. This is the general market trend. Movements are rapid. When you are new to any type of trading market, identifying trends is an effective strategy.

A trend for long-term traders lasts a few days to months. They will occupy the position for several days, weeks, or months. In contrast, a day trader or scalper in cryptocurrencies would not do so. A day trader will actively "ride the waves" both up and down, and then depart the market within minutes or hours.

If you have chosen to engage in frequent trades, identifying dips will provide you with a superior entry point when a mini-rally has begun. This will be your initial course of action.

Observe the graphical representation of price movements as you commence. The numbers are unimportant, so don't worry too much about them. These numbers cannot provide an accurate depiction of the price as it takes shape. Observe the chart and modify the timescale to 5 seconds, 10 seconds, and 1 minute to determine the movement's nature. Observe how every advance is followed by a retracement and every decline is halted by an abrupt increase. You must become accustomed to this type of pattern and employ it when purchasing the dip.

However, you should never place an order when the market shifts from one trend to another. You should wait for the price to drop, then acquire it on its subsequent rise. This enables you to observe the rally formation rather than immediately confronting the retracements. This also permits you to affirm the forward push. You can use market declines as a signal to enter the market.

When organizing the market, you should also wait for a downturn. At this juncture, the dip takes on an entirely new meaning; it is temporarily reversing its downward trend and climbing. Do not engage too quickly. Attend to it. When it reaches its peak and begins to descend is the ideal time to capture it. Never attempt to capture it at its height.

In the short term, it will result in a perfect capture, but in the long run it will be inferior.

The apex and the trough each serve a unique purpose, and that purpose is not to harvest or liquidate, but to plan your next move. Your trigger locations should be the peak and the valley.

Arbitrage

Beginners should promptly attempt to learn and comprehend this advanced strategy. Arbitrage is not concerned with the up and down fluctuations of the market, but rather with the mispricing of the market. This is an underutilized crypto trading strategy. If you only take away one thing from this entire book, make it this strategy.

When there are a large number of possible combinations, it is best to use automated programs because, without automation, you won't be able to take advantage of cryptocurrencies' greatest benefit – tradability and volatility.

With arbitrage, you will seek out price disparities between pairings.

For example, there is the price of A relative to B, the price of B relative to C, and the price of C relative to A. If everything goes as planned and the A: B ratio is 1:2 and the B: C ratio is!:3, then the A: C price should be 1:6. A bids 1:6:5 in a pricing mismatch, using the same example. Why is this so? It's basic. In exchange for 1 unit of A used to purchase C, you can receive 6:5. With 6:5, C can be used to acquire B at a price of 1:3, resulting in 2.167 B. You convert the 2.167 units of B back into A to obtain 1.08 units of A. Therefore, you began the arbitrage exercise with 1 unit of A and left with 1.08 units of A.

This is an example of an 8% return, which is irrelevant because the numbers are merely examples. Arbitrage trading is advantageous because it requires only 30 seconds to execute a trade.

Now let's look at how you can implement this in your trading. You should keep in mind that on any given day, there will be numerous opportunities for mispricing, and it will be difficult to capture them all manually. However, you'll need a program or an AI algorithm to capture them and conduct your trades. Simply keep the program operating and configure it to trade automatically or seek approval before initiating trades.

If you are unable to do this, there are many other traders who will. Whoever completes it the quickest obtains a prize.

The merchants utilizing web-based portals would not be able to acquire it. You'll need an exceedingly low-latency system and real-time data feeds to take advantage of this. You will have a greater possibility of success if you are using a T1 line and Bloomberg Terminal.

On Balance Volume

This third trading strategy goes beyond purchasing and selling whenever the trader desires. The first strategy, purchasing the dips, is designed to allow you to identify market entry and exit triggers. On a deeper level, the objective is to familiarize you with the nature of price fluctuations and the use of charts to visualize them. On the other hand, arbitrage was ostensibly designed to help you take advantage of market mispricing. On a deeper level, this second strategy broadens your perspective on the ways you can profit from the markets.

Now, the balance volume is intended to reveal what the intelligent money is doing. This third strategy allows you to track where all the money is accruing. If you can familiarize yourself with the movements of large sums of money, you can easily leverage trends and capitalize on fluctuations.

This requires an OBV (on balance volume) indicator. It is available on Bloomberg Terminal. a number of prominent MT4 for cryptos also offer it.

The OBV indicator provides insight into the amount of capital flowing into each position. Seeing where the money is going enables you to anticipate when it will take off. This is not typically displayed on online or web-based trading platforms. With OBV, you have a "better view" of the market's direction at any given time.

You can also observe when the market begins to decline, enabling you to exit a position, swap counters, or short the asset. With OBV, you can analyze the market and determine what to do when you begin to feel comfortable. You must attentively monitor two things: pending trades and OBV.

You must also be aware of the OBV mismatch, which is a second-order trade – you will no longer look at the prices to determine the trade, but rather at the effect of the surrounding activity, which is measured by the OBV.

When you identify a mismatch between two cryptocurrencies, you must examine their transaction prices to determine whether the prices are converging or diverging. If the price is converging, prepare a sell order. If it is diverging, then the opposite should be done.

The following chapter will cover trading indicators.

A Brief Overview Of Cryptocurrency

In the prehistoric era, people utilized the barter system, in which two or more individuals exchange goods and services. For instance, one can substitute seven pears for seven oranges. The widespread abandonment of the barter system was due to three obvious flaws:

If you have something to trade, someone else must also want it, and you must also want what the other party is offering.

There is no universal criterion for determining value; rather, you must determine how many of your possessions you are willing to trade for other items. Not all items are divisible. A living mammal, for example, cannot be divided into smaller segments.

The items cannot be transmitted easily, unlike our current currency, which can be stored on a mobile phone or in a wallet. As it became apparent that the barter system was ineffective, a number of modifications were made to the monetary system: in 110 B.C., an official currency was established; in A.D., coins were introduced. In 1250, the first gold-plated florins were issued and disseminated throughout Europe. From 1600 to 1900, paper currency acquired widespread acceptance and was utilized globally. This is the history of the creation of modern currency as we know it.

Examples of modern money include paper currency, coinage, credit cards, and digital wallets such as Apple Pay, Amazon Pay, and PayPal, among others. There is a single regulatory body that supervises the operation of paper currency and credit cards, which is supervised by banks and governments.

conventional versus electronic currency

Consider a scenario in which you wish to reimburse a friend who purchased you lunch via an online payment to their account. There are several potential negative consequences, including:

The financial institution may be experiencing a technical issue, such as a system outage or equipment malfunction.

There is a chance that the account you or an acquaintance are using has been compromised, for example, by a denial-of-service attack or impersonation.

It is conceivable that your or your friend's account transfer limits have been reached. The bank is the primary failure site.

Therefore, cryptocurrencies are the future form of currency. Imagine a comparable transaction between two users of the bitcoin application. A notification prompts the user to confirm that they are prepared to send bitcoins. If so, processing will start: The system verifies the user's identity, verifies that they have sufficient funds to complete the transaction, etc. The funds are then deposited into the recipient's account after the payment has been transmitted. This procedure requires a few minutes to complete.

Since there are no limits on the amount that can be transferred, your accounts cannot be hacked, and there is no singular point of failure, cryptocurrency overcomes all of the shortcomings of modern banking. As previously stated, there are currently more than 1,600 cryptocurrencies in circulation; notable examples include Bitcoin, Litecoin, Ethereum, and Zcash. Additionally, every day a new cryptocurrency is created. Given the present rate of expansion, it is highly probable that there will be much more to come.

Let's discuss what cryptocurrency is currently.

What exactly is Cryptocurrency?

A cryptocurrency is a string of encrypted information that represents a unit of currency.

Blockchains are peer-to-peer networks that function as secure transaction ledgers while also monitoring and coordinating bitcoin activities such as purchasing and selling.

Using encryption technology, cryptocurrencies can function as a form of payment and an accounting system.

Cryptocurrency refers to any digital or virtual currency used for commercial transactions.

Although it has some similarities to traditional currency, it lacks a corporeal form and requires encryption to function. Since there is no central bank or governing body that regulates the operation of cryptocurrencies, new units can only be created if certain conditions are satisfied.

In the case of Bitcoin, for example, the miner is compensated in bitcoins only after a block has been published to the blockchain, and this is the only way new bitcoins can be created.

Bitcoins are limited to a maximum supply of 21 million, after which no more will be created.

The benefits of cryptocurrencies

Transferability:

Cryptocurrency makes transacting with individuals on the opposite side of the globe as simple as going grocery shopping in your neighborhood.

You are not required to provide any additional personal information when making a purchase with cryptocurrency.

This indicates that banks, payment systems, advertisers, and credit-rating agencies should not have access to your financial information. Because no sensitive information is required to be transmitted over the internet, there is a minimal risk that your bank information or identity will be stolen.

Almost all cryptocurrencies, including Bitcoin, Ethereum, Tezos, and Bitcoin Cash, are protected by a technique known as a blockchain, which is routinely checked and affirmed by a substantial amount of computing power.

Your bitcoin assets are accessible no matter where you are on the planet or what happens to any of the main intermediaries in the global banking system, as they are not tied to a financial institution or government.

On the Bitcoin, Ethereum, Tezos, and Bitcoin Cash networks, each and every transaction is always made public.

This suggests that there is no room for manipulating transactions, the money supply, or the rules of a game in the midst of play.

In contrast to payments made with credit cards, cryptocurrency transactions are irreversible.

This reduces the likelihood of fraud for business proprietors significantly. By eliminating one of the primary justifications given by credit card issuers for their excessive processing fees, the transaction costs for consumers could be reduced.

Safety: The Bitcoin network has never been compromised. Due to the permissionless nature of the systems and the open-source nature of the core software, innumerable computer scientists and cryptographers have been able to analyze every aspect of the networks' security, thereby contributing to the safety of cryptocurrencies.

What is cryptography?

Cryptography is the use of encryption and decryption in the presence of third parties with malicious intent, such as third parties seeking to steal your data or eavesdrop on your conversation.

In cryptography, both a public key, which functions as the user's shared digital identity, and a private key, which functions as the user's confidential digital signature, are utilized. SHA-256 is the hashing algorithm utilized by Bitcoin. In a typical bitcoin transaction, the transaction information, such as who you wish to send the bitcoins to and how many you wish to send, appears first.

The information is then processed with a hashing algorithm. As indicated, Bitcoin uses the SHA-256 algorithm. The user's private key, which is used to uniquely identify the user, is then employed to sign the result prior to its transmission. After being digitally authenticated, the result is then sent over the network for other users to verify. Using the sender's public key accomplishes this.

Miners are responsible for determining whether a transaction is valid or not. After this stage is complete, the transaction and several others are uploaded to the blockchain, where data cannot be altered. Given its complexity, it is plausible to assert that the encryption is extremely challenging to crack.

How To Begin Investing In Cryptosurrensu

coinbase is the cryptocurrency exchange with the highest growth rate. It has reached the tenth position among the top volume sryrtosurrensu exchanges in a mere five months. The popularity of Binance can be attributed to a number of factors, including its availability in multiple languages, its user-friendly interface, and its ability to process orders at an extremely rapid rate. Binance exchange is only accessible for trading purposes; therefore, it is not available for any wired FIAT transactions.

Should I create a Coinbase Account?

If coinbase continues to expand at its current rate, it will soon become the largest cryptocurrency exchange for trading altcoins worldwide. Many newly launched cryptocurrencies and tokens are being listed on Binance alongside the other major exchanges (Poloniex and Bittrex). If you missed some ICOs, you can search for them on the Binance exchange.

BNB is the name of the cryptocurrency created by coinbase. It is an optional method for calculating the exchange fees, which consist of the following: Trading fees associated with purchasing or selling bitcoin, as well as listing and withdrawal fees.

When using BNB coins, you will receive a 50% discount on the first year of your account, 25% on the second year, 12.5% on the third year, and 6.25% on the fourth year.

BNB tokens are also utilized for coinbase e Launchpad, which is a way to invest in specific ICOs on coinbase. These ICOs will be listed on the Binance exchange's next ICO listing.

coinbase intends to use 20% of its revenue to acquire BNB from the open market.

The rrose for getting started trading cryptocurrencies is simple, but there are a few important notes to comprehend (similar to what was stated previously, but this time pertaining to using binance).

Sign up for Coinbase first.com

Register with Coinbase.Create a digital currency wallet where you can store digital currency securely.

Connect your bank account, debit card, or credit card so that you can convert and withdraw digital currency.

Invest in Bitcoin, Ethereum, and/or Litecoin (exchanging U.S. dollars for srurtosurrensu).

Sell Bitcoin, Ethereum, and/or Litecoin for srurtosurrensu in exchange for US dollars.

Consider registering for another exchange and trading srurtosurrensu for srurtosurrensu (and then transferring that back into Bitsoin, Ethereum, and/or

Litecoin, then back into coinbase, and then basking it into USD). Don't neglect to report your transactions to the tax man and review your tax imrlisation (this cannot be stressed enough).

The advantage of having a USD wallet on Coinbase.Some i that you can put money in and then use to purchase coins immediately. If you use your bank account to purchase real estate, the transaction can take up to a week. A credit card does not have this problem, but its limits are typically lower. TIP: When using Coinbase to purchase, I don't always deposit USD in my wallet as opposed to buying coins directly from Binance using my bank account (I do this on the go). You can also transmit money if the funds must be in the uisker wallet. Consequently, I almost always use GDAX to buy and sell cryptocurrency when I'm using a desktop computer (using Binance for my wallet and mobile device).

You do not need to purchase an entire coin. You can purchase soin in fractions.

Bitcoins are expensive in 2018, so if you don't have a large bankroll, consider purchasing fractions of a coin to commence. It has historically been a mistake to purchase only ETH and LTC, as BTC is significantly more valuable. Buying all three coins for the same amount of money (regardless of how many of each coin that buys) is one way to prevent making a poor investment decision based on price tag per coin.

When purchasing a coin, you should take a breath and examine the information. An additional decimal point can result in large sums of money, as a single Bitcoin can trade for over $4,000 $10,000. $14,000 – $20,000.

Install the app. This allows you trade srurtosurrensu from uour rhone. The market is volatile and transactions are sluggish; therefore, when it's time to buy or sell, you must act immediately.

Set notifications. Alerts can assist you in determining when to buy or sell.

There is a feature that permits incremental purchases over time. Averaging a position on a weekly basis is a time-saving strategy that Coinbase automates for you.

Crurtosurrensu is volatile! There is always a chance that the market will crash, or that you will experience some other disaster. Crurtosurrensu is not a fiat surrensu that is centrally controlled and regulated. There is essentially nothing you can do if you lose a token or someone exploits you, which is why you need two-factor authentication.

In other words, trading cryptocurrencies is simple to begin, but there are a few crucial concepts to grasp before you begin trading with a wallet-exchange such as Coinbase.

Last but not least, there are a few other options for setting up your wallet and exchanging currency. The majority, however, will rair with a Coinbase account, making it an excellent starting point.

Few CrurtoTrade regulations exist.

Select the appropriate trading platform.

Timing is crucial. Wait for the next orrortunitu if you miss.

In business, there will always be ups and downs. Buy in Bearish market. sell in Bull Market.

Understand the srurto vocabulary.

For long-term srurto storage. Know the company, its founder, and its personnel. Total soins. Its development roadblocks

Only Purchase Valuable Coins

Never sell a coin that is in profit when it is in loss. Only sell a portion of your position

Never Listen Trollboxes

Don't Invest All Your Money In A Single Coin

DIFFERENCE BETWEEN BITCOIN AND ETHEREUM

Ethereum, like Bitcoin, is an open-source blockchain network. Although there are some differences between them, the most important distinction is that they have different roles.

Bitcoin offers a specialized implementation of blockchain technology and was created as a career-to-career tool that facilitates digital transactions. Ethereum, on the other hand, is a platform for executing transactions on a decentralized network that enables intelligent comparisons between individuals worldwide.

HOW TO BEGIN INVESTING IN BITCOIN AND ETH

There are multiple methods to invest in virtual securities, depending on your preferences. Here are the fundamentals of purchasing and investing in Bitcoin and Ethereum.

Coinbase

If you are new to cryptocurrencies, the best way to get started is with Bitcoin.

Coinbase is an online platform for exchanging, buying, selling, and storing cryptocurrencies. Its creators desired to develop an oren system that would enable users to convert digital to analog signals.

Its benefits

It makes buying and selling digital currency simple.

You need not be concerned about esurtu or baskur.

One interface encompasses everything you require, from wallet to exchange to merchant tool.

How does it work?

Establish an Account

Visit coinbase.com and access your account. After updating your email address, you can access the Buy/Sell Option Sequence. Before you can rurshae any Btson, however, you must take a few more ter.

Verify Your Checking Account

You will be required to connect your bank account to Coinbase. This amount allows you to convert US dollars to British pounds. Conbae will verify your bank account to ensure that everything is secure.

Verify Your Telephone Number

When logging into your Coinbase account, you will be required to enter a password and a security token sent to your mobile device. No one else will be able to access your account after this point. Conbae will also verify your phone number as an additional security measure.

Invest in Your First Betsy

Now that everything has been released, you can access the Buy Bitcoin page and enter the desired amount. If you wish to sell Bitcoins, you must navigate to the Sell section, enter the quantity, select the wallet from which you wish to sell, and then select the amount you wish to deposit the coins. The only remaining step is to confirm the order.

For Ethereum; There are a number of online platforms you can use to purchase Ethereum. Coinbase is one of the most trustworthy platforms for purchasing and storing digital currency in an electronic wallet. It is avalable to users in over 30 countries, including the United States, the United Kingdom, Canada, Singapore, and the following Eurorean countries: Austria, Belgium, Bulgaria, Croatia, Cyprus, Czech Republic, Denmark, Finland, France, Germany, Hungary, Ireland, Italy, Latvia, Lithuania, Luxembourg, Malta, Monaco, the Netherlands, Norway, Poland,

Portugal, Romania, San Marino, and Slovakia.

Coinbase account creation.

The initial step is to create a Coinbase account. This will provide you with a secure location to store your Ether and simple methods to convert your local currency into or out of digital currency.

Join accounts.

Your Bank Account, Credit Card, or Debit Card Number. After you sign ur, sonnest uour bank assount, sredit sard or debit sard. Before you can use the account, you'll need to pass some verification steps. Once the verification steps have been completed, you may initiate a search.

Sell and buy.

Purchase and sell Ether. After starting your first purchase, Coinbase will complete your buy and deliver your

Ethereum. (Sells work in the same manner but with more reverence. The price of Ether changes over time, so Coinbase will show you the current exchange rate before you buy.

www.ingramcontent.com/pod-product-compliance
Lightning Source LLC
Chambersburg PA
CBHW050255120526
44590CB00016B/2358